LUMBINI to KUSHINARA

by

Varsha Uke Nagpal

Copyright © 2016 Varsha Uke Nagpal

All rights reserved. This book or any portion thereof may not be reproduced or used in any manner whatsoever without the express written permission of the author except for the use of brief quotations in a book review.

DISCLAIMER

This is a work of creative nonfiction. The events are portrayed to the best of my knowledge and is based on my personal understanding of the historical interpretations. While all the stories in this book are believed to be true, there is no hard core historical evidence of the events having actually happened in the manner narrated in this book. I do not assume and hereby disclaim any liability to any party for any loss, damage, or disruption caused by errors or omissions, whether such errors or omissions result from negligence, accident, or any other cause. This book does not claim to be a religious text for Buddhism, but depicts only the life of Gautama Buddha

LUMBINI to KUSHINARA

Dedicated to the memory of my father
NG Uke.

Thank you Kamal Uke, my mother, for
inculcating the love of History in me

Written for
Kunaal, Aaliya and Aaria

Varsha Uke Nagpal

ACKNOWLEDGEMENTS

This book would not have been possible without the constant support, encouragement, inputs and immense patience of Triloki Nath Nagpal, my best friend forever…

Thank you Aaria Nagpal, my granddaughter for the beautiful painting of the omnipresent sun which I thought captured what Buddhism is today. Aaria is 7 years old and her painting adorns the cover of this book.

Thank you Chaitali Hireker, Anurag Nagpal, Jharna Madan, Sunil Uke & Neena Gulati for your suggestions, encouragement and support.

Varsha Uke Nagpal

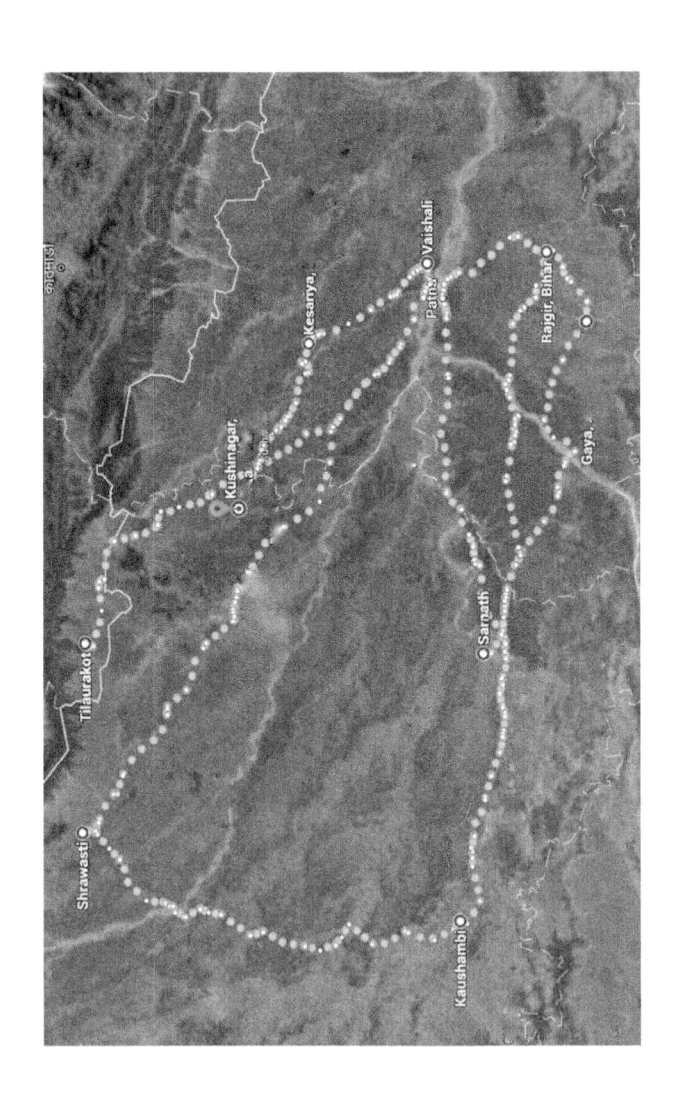

BUDDHA'S PATH

CONTENTS

	Page
Prologue	9
Geneological Table	15
1. Lumbini	17
2. Kapilvastu	25
3. Bodhgaya	35
4. Sarnath	43
5. Rajgrih	61
6. Nalanda	69
7. Vaishali	79
8. Kesariya	89
9. Shrawasti	95

10. Kaushambi — 105

11. Kushinara — 113

12. Sanchi — 121

13. Patliputra — 127

14. Buddha's Countenance — 133

15. 6th Century BC — 137

Epilogue — 143

Buddhist Sangiti — 147

Sixteen Ganarajyas — 153

First Disciples of Buddha — 155

Reference Maps — 155

Glossary — 157

LUMBINI to KUSHINARA

PROLOGUE

As a child I had been to Bodh Gaya, Rajgir, Nalanda and Sarnath a couple of times. My father was fond of travelling and visiting places of historical importance. He made sure that we visited all these places with him. My mother was fond of History, so she would tell us all about the place that we visited. At that time, I saw the places, ran amongst the ruins, climbed numerous steps, and walked between monasteries that existed about 2600 years ago. As time passed by I grew older, I retired from my job and had plenty of time to travel. I decided to revisit the places that were connected with the life and times of Siddharth Gautam who went on to become the Buddha. I wanted to see de novo the places and tread the path that Buddha took on his journey from Lumbini to Kushinara. I wanted to see the path that he traversed in the eighty years that he spent on Earth.

Now as an adult when I visited all these places, every place left a new impression on me. I was delighted to be walking on the path that Siddharth walked on so many years ago. The uppermost question on my mind was, "What was this place like 2600 years ago when Siddharth left Kapilvastu in his quest for knowledge?"

I started imagining the place as a large forest with nothing but trees, perhaps free roaming animals, no semblance of comfort, no house and no shelter from the elements. It was simply "solitude in the wilderness". In those circumstances, Siddharth lived for days on end practicing yogic meditation and seeking answers from within himself. Once he received answers to his queries, he sought out those who had till then been with him. Those five ascetics led by Kaundinya had since left him as they thought that he had gone astray and had deviated from strict penance and torture of the body.

Therefore, in the beginning it was one man with knowledge, then five more joined him, then fifty-five. The number kept increasing, more followers joined in until his knowledge spread, his mission became bigger and soon this philosophy started taking on the form of a religion. The Buddha died but his philosophy lives on.

The journey of this philosophy over thousands of years, added to the story of the Buddha. A lot of myths and stories started doing the rounds. Sometimes these stories were propagated by vested interests to undermine the persona that Siddharth was. Sometimes it was spread to show that the Buddha believed in miracles, rebirth and many other superstitious beliefs.

Buddha had told his followers never to accept any doctrine or philosophy without asking questions, he asked his followers to question and seek answers and only after getting convinced, then accept what anyone said.

Could any person have lived a life of seclusion for 29 years without knowing anything about illness, old age and death? It would be possible if that person lived isolated away from society, but we have been told that Siddharth lived in a palace surrounded by people. There is a story told about a bird that was injured by his cousin Devdutt, then how would Siddharth not have known of pain, suffering and injury?

I therefore do not agree that he was kept secluded till the age of 29, when having seen old age and death he decided to run away from the world. I cannot agree with the story that Siddharth fled from his house leaving a wife and young child to fend for themselves. There had to be something more realistic in Siddharth's world.

I have tried to understand his quest, his journey, his life and his travels. I have tried to see what life would have been like then, I have tried to feel those places, see those visions, and understand the importance of those places. This journey of mine, my thoughts are presented here for your reading and understanding what Siddharth Gautam Buddha was all about.

LUMBINI to KUSHINARA

When you visit Bodhgaya, sit under the tree, close your eyes and try to visualize what could have gone on in the mind of a young person seeking some answers from the universe. I would suggest to you, my reader, to be with your own self, allow your mind to be free, just feel the energy of the place and feel peace surround you. Set yourself on a journey away from the 21st century and go all the way back into 6th century BC.

I do hope your journey will be more than a holiday, where we tick off one box after the other. May your journey lead you to understand, that there was once upon a time a man, who just like us walked on earth, sought answers and left behind him a legacy for eternity.

Varsha Uke Nagpal

LUMBINI to KUSHINARA

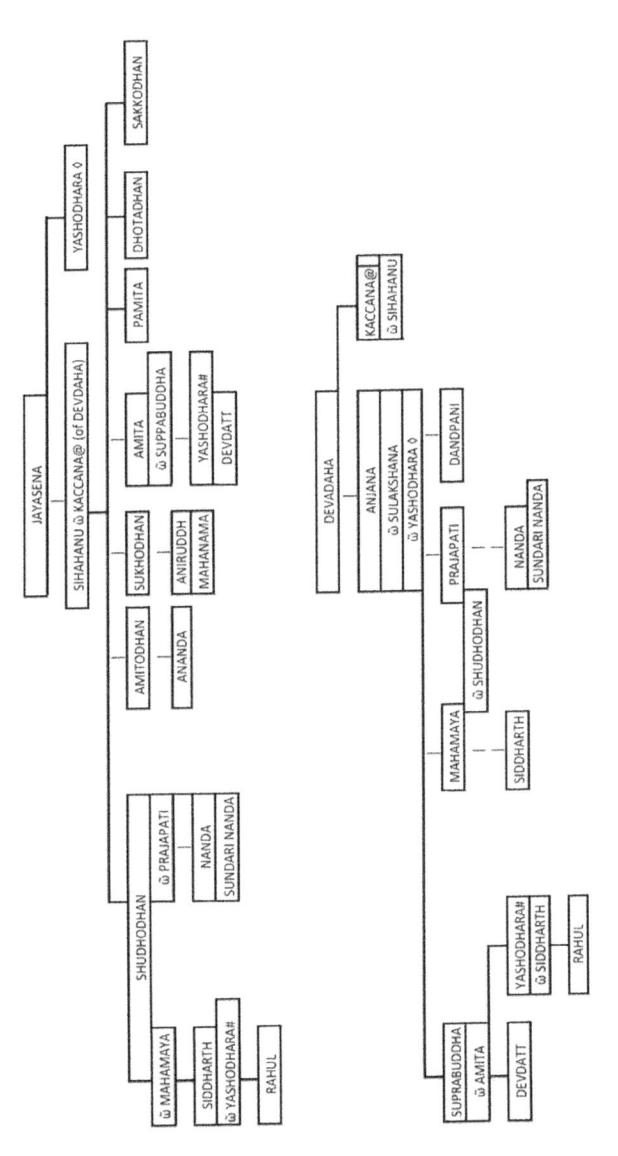

GENEOLOGICAL TABLE

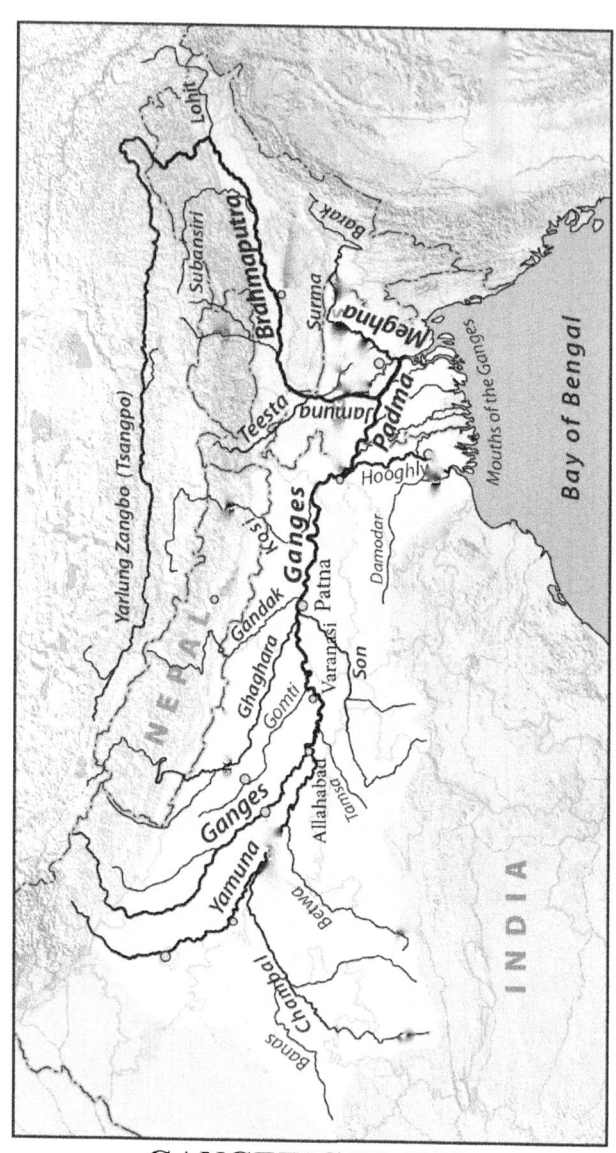

GANGETIC PLAIN

1

LUMBINI

Many years ago at the time of my story, the sun, the moon, the stars and the sky were just as they are today. The earth even then kept rotating on its own axis and the days and nights kept changing just as regularly. The earth kept revolving around the sun in its own orbit and the seasons kept changing regularly.

The Himalayas stood on guard as sentinels protecting this huge land mass which we call Bharat or India. On the south of this landmass of India are huge volumes of water. There is the Bay of Bengal on the east, the Arabian Sea on the west and the southern most tip has the huge Indian Ocean. The Ganga and the Yamuna rivers originated from the beautiful snow-capped mountains of the Himalayas. *"Himalaya"* means the abode of snow. Those huge mountains are always covered with snow, and the rivers come down gushing over the plains of the north of this huge landmass of India and bring prosperity to the land through which they travel.

Great settlements came around these rivers. Over time a system evolved, and customs and traditions started getting formulated. The region from where these rivers passed were called the *Terai* or wetlands. There was abundance of water and the rivers brought with them silt from all the areas that they crossed on their way to their destination, which was the Bay of Bengal in the east of India. Beautiful cities and great civilizations developed along the banks of these two rivers. Prayag, Varanasi, Pataliputra were prominent cities on the banks of the Ganga.

In those days there were small states which were called *Ganarajyas. Gana* means clan and *rajya* means rule. In Northern India there were sixteen *Ganarajyas* then, where each had a King who was elected by the people to rule for a fixed period. The King was advised by eminent advisors on matters of governance. These Kings were male heads of families belonging to the *kshatriya* clan.

Interestingly in Greece, around the same time in 507 BC, an Athenian leader Cleisthenes introduced a system of political reforms that was called "Demokratia" or Rule by the people. Yes indeed, the word Democracy is derived from this Greek word. In Athens too the ruler was elected by male citizens of Athens who were over the age of eighteen.

My story belongs to the 6th century BC, which is about 2600 years ago. In those days, at the foothills of the mighty Himalayas, towards the east of India, there was a state called Kapilvastu and its capital was at Tilaurakot. This area today is in Nepal. The ruling clan of this state were the Shakyas and the name of the King at that time was Shudhodhan. He had two wives, one was Mahamaya and the second was Prajapati Gautami. These two girls were sisters and belonged to the Koliya clan which ruled at Devdaha, also in Nepal today. In those days marriage within relatives was common and so we find that these two sisters were the daughters of King Shudhodhan's paternal aunt. Both these Kingdoms were vassal states of the Kingdom of Kosala. Kosala was the area which today is called Shrawasti, towards the north of Uttar Pradesh in India.

In the month of Vaishakh, which would correspond to the month of May according to the Gregorian calendar, Queen Mahamaya left Tilaurakot to go to her parental home at Devdaha, to give birth to her child. She stopped on the way to rest at a forest called Lumbini which was about twenty-seven kilometres from Kapilvastu. She still had to travel thirty-five kilometres north east of Lumbini to reach Devdaha. In this Lumbini forest on *Vaishakh Purnima*, a son was born to the Queen under a *saal* tree. The saal today is also known as Sakhua, Shala or Shorea Robusta.

There was a pond near this tree which was called Pushkarni. It is said that Mahamaya took her bath at this pond and after seven days of the birth of her child,

Mahamaya died. The child who was named Siddharth was brought up by his step mother Prajapati Gautami, and was also called Gautam.

PUSHKARNI AT LUMBINI

Today in the 21st century, Lumbini has become a pilgrimage place. There is a temple built over the spot where Siddharth was born. When I visited this temple, I found that there was a long but orderly queue of people who had come to see the place. One could stand peacefully as long as one wished to, there was no jostling, no pushing, everyone waited patiently to take their turn to venerate the spot. After all, everyone had come from far away to see the place, so everyone was allowed freedom to stand as long as they wished to.

LUMBINI TEMPLE

One could see the stump of a tree which may have stood there 2600 years ago, as that place has now been covered with glass. To maintain the sanctity of Lumbini, a large area has been cordoned off and is maintained as a beautiful garden. No commercial activity is allowed inside these gardens. Temples have been built here by Buddhists from Thailand, Sri Lanka and some more Buddhist countries.

There are a lot of ruins of ancient monasteries, stupas and layers of brick structures in this area. These ruins belong to a time which was much after the death of Buddha, it belongs to the 3rd century BC, when Emperor Ashoka ruled over a very large area of India.

LOTUS POND

On both sides of the road leading to Lumbini are beautiful water bodies filled with Lotus flowers. Being in Lumbini, going back 2600 years and imagining the times of the Buddha is a very surreal feeling.

Lumbini is the best place to start your journey to know more about the times of the Buddha, as the journey of Siddharth had begun here, 2600 years ago.

Varsha Uke Nagpal

2

KAPILVASTU

As Siddharth was the son of a King and belonged to the *kshatriya* caste, he was taught all the skills that a prince and a person of the warrior caste needs to know. When he was of marriageable age, which in those days was around sixteen, he was married to Princess Yashodhara who was also called Bhaddakaccana. She was the daughter of Siddharth's maternal uncle of the Koliya clan of Devdaha. They had a son who was named Rahul.

Both Kapilvastu and Devdaha were *Ganarajyas*. The Kings of the *Ganarajya* were elected by the people and it was not a hereditary title. In those days there used to be an institution called a *Santhagar*, which literally means, santha+agar, or group+house or assembly place. In these *Santhagars* general assembly of old and young men of a clan was held regularly and decisions on matters of general and state affairs were taken by consensus. The *Ganarajyas* or Republic states used to control relations with other states and also took decisions on matters of war and peace. The minimum age for joining the *Santhagar* was twenty. Siddharth was a member of the *Santhagar* and would actively participate in decision making.

When Siddharth was twenty-nine years old, a dispute came up before the Assembly regarding sharing of waters of the River Rohini which flowed between the areas that belonged to the Koliyas as well as the Shakyas. The river water was shared by both the clans for irrigation purpose. As a dispute arose, the majority in the *Santhagar* were in favour of waging a war against the Koliyas to solve the problem once and for all.

Siddharth was opposed to war, as he thought that war did not solve problems. He suggested peaceful negotiations to end the conflict, but most of the members of the *Santhagar* did not agree with the suggestion of Siddharth. It was decided by majority vote that the Shakyas would declare war on the Koliyas. It was also decided that all young men of the *Santhagar* would need to join in the war.

As Siddharth disagreed with this proposal, he did not agree to join the war. The leaders of the *Santhagar* told him that if he did not join the war, then there were three alternatives available to him. He could either (1) join the war, or (2) offer himself to go in exile or (3) allow his family to face social boycott, with confiscation of their property.

The Shakyas were vassals of the King of Kosala, therefore permission would have to be taken from the King to punish Siddharth. The presumption was that the King of Kosala would not be inclined to agree with the proposal of sending Siddharth to exile or confiscate the family property.

The only solution available to Siddharth therefore was to choose the second alternative as that would cause least problems for his family. Siddharth therefore offered to become a *parivrajaka* and take self-imposed exile, with the permission of his parents as well as his wife.

Although Siddharth's parents were heart broken by this decision, but after Siddharth convinced them, they agreed to let him go. Yashodhara his wife, understood the problem and agreed with Siddharth that there was no other alternative but for Siddharth to become a *parivrajaka*, and she also agreed to his proposal.

As Siddharth had taken self-inflicted exile he had to leave the Kingdom of Kapilvastu. Siddharth chose to leave from the East gate of the palace from which he went up to the River Rohini in his chariot driven by Channa. At the banks of the river he removed his royal robes as well as jewellery and gave them to Channa his charioteer to take back to his father King Shudhodhan. His horse Kanthka, returned with the chariot and Channa, but did not enter the palace gates. He died just outside the gate of the palace. Kapilvastu today is located in western part of Nepal.

STUPA AT KUDAN

At Tilaurakot, the capital of Kapilvastu, today there are ruins of the palace said to have been the place where Siddharth spent twenty-nine years of his life. The ruins are of two gates, and a few palaces. The place is not maintained very well, but one can make out that once upon a time there was a lovely palace here.

There are two stupa like structures, near the ruins of the palace, which are supposed to be the place where Siddharth's parents Shudhodhan and his wife were cremated.

About 7 Kms. away from Tilaurakot is a town called Kudan which was then called Nigrodharama. This is the place where Shudhodhan went to meet Buddha, when he visited Kapilvastu for the first time after attaining enlightenment. It is also the place where Rahul met his father for the first time after he became the Buddha. At that time Rahul was seven years old. As prompted by Yashodhara his mother, Rahul asked his father for his inheritance. Buddha then allowed Rahul to enter the *Sangh* as a *samner* or a novice. On hearing that Rahul would join the *Sangh*, Shudhodhan was upset and told Buddha that in future no child should be allowed to enter the *Sangh* without the permission of his parents or guardians. As Siddharth had renounced the world and become an ascetic, he did not have a right over Rahul, and therefore Shudhodhan felt that permission should have been taken from him who was the guardian and head of the family of Rahul. This suggestion was accepted by Buddha.

In India in UP at a place called Piprahwa, ruins of palaces have also been found and claims are made that this is the real Kapilvastu where Prince Siddharth lived 2600 years ago.

PIPRAHWA

From Kapilvastu when I visited Piprahwa which is in India, we had to take a very convoluted route, but at the end of it I found that actually Tilaurakot and Piprahwa are not very far from each other, and are now divided by the border of Nepal and India.

2600 years ago there was no such border and the palaces and the city could have been spread across to cover both Tilaurakot and Piprahwa.

After leaving Kapilvastu and crossing the river Rohini, Siddharth wandered from place to place trying to find a good teacher so that he could increase his knowledge and find solutions to problems in his mind.

RIVER ROHINI

When he reached the town of Vaishali, which was the capital of the Vajjian *Ganarajya*, he met Alara Kalam a resident of Vaishali who was a teacher of Yogic Meditation and belonged originally to a nearby place called Kesariya. Siddharth learnt a *dhyanic* state called the sphere of nothingness from Alara Kalam who became his first teacher. Having mastered this form of meditation, Siddharth moved on and found his next teacher Uddaka Ramaputta. Uddaka too was a meditator and taught Siddharth refined state of meditation known as material attainments or the sphere of neither perception nor non perception. After mastering both these forms of Meditation, Siddharth moved further south and reached Rajgrih which was the capital of the Magadh Empire. The ruler of Magadh in those days was Bimbisar who knew that Siddharth was from Kapilvastu and had taken self imposed exile. He therefore invited Siddharth to stay in Rajgrih, because an exile from one Kingdom could live in another Kingdom. As Siddharth wanted to increase his knowledge and seek solutions to problems, he did not accept this invitation to stay at one place.

He joined a group of five ascetics led by Kaundinya and tried to find enlightenment through deprivation of worldly goods and by practising self mortification. He tried penance, starved himself, lived on roots and did all the things possible to torture his body to attain knowledge and salvation. It was thought in those days that one could attain salvation by torturing one's body. The ascetics would find new ways to perform penance, and torture their body so that they would be able to find what they were seeking from life.

3

BODHGAYA

Siddharth along with Kaundinya and four other mendicants kept moving from place to place and practicing meditation and penance. They kept wandering, seeking teachers and adopting different ways and means to seek answers to their questions. After about six years of having left Kapilvastu, Siddharth reached the banks of the river Niranjana.

On the banks of this river there is a major Hindu pilgrimage town called Gaya. The literal translation of the word *gaya* is gone. Gaya is the place of salvation for all Hindus. According to followers of Hinduism there is a concept of rebirth after death. Traditionally, after the death of a person the last rites are performed by his family members to enable him to get freedom from this eternal cycle of life and death. To get salvation, it is believed that if the last rites or *Shradh* of a person is conducted at Gaya then his soul would rest in peace forever as all the sins of all the ancestors of the person performing the *Shradh* at Gaya would be absolved.

RIVER NIRANJANA

On *Vaishakha Purnima* day, as Siddharth sat under a *Peepal* tree meditating for almost forty-nine days, a lady named

Sujata who lived in Village Senani near Uruvela (old name of Gaya) across the river Niranjana, came near the tree. Following some religious tradition, Sujata had come to offer *Kheer* (Rice Pudding) to the *Vriksh Devata* (Tree God). Siddharth who had been fasting for the last 49 days, ate the offered *Kheer* and then it is said enlightenment dawned upon him.

He realized that extreme asceticism did not work. His thoughts crystallised and he discovered a path of moderation away from extreme self indulgence and self mortification. He realised that torturing the body by starvation and practicing extreme penance did not help. It became evident to him that everything in moderation led to success in achieving goals.

He could then propound the Middle path, which he called the "*Ashtang Marg*" or the eight-fold path. "The *Ashtang Marg*" briefly is Right belief, Right thought, Right speech, Right action, Right livelihood, Right effort, Right mindfulness, Right meditation.

After becoming enlightened, Siddharth who had now become the Buddha, looked for the five ascetics who were with him when he had started meditating at Gaya. He wanted to share his new found philosophy with them. These five ascetics meanwhile had left Gaya as they thought that Siddharth had strayed from asceticism as he had broken his penance by partaking of the *Kheer*.

My journey in the 21st century to Gaya was complete when I reached the tree under which Siddharth sat to meditate and where he became enlightened.

The original tree under which Siddharth sat 2600 years ago, is no longer alive, but the present one planted at the same spot is a sapling of the original tree.

In 288 BC, Emperor Ashoka (304-232 BC) sent a sapling of the original tree to Srilanka, then called Tamraparni, with his son Mahendra and daughter Sanghamitra. That tree flourished in Srilanka and a number of saplings from that tree were sent to many places for plantation in Srilanka as well as in India.

Emperor Ashoka had embraced Buddhism after the Kalinga War in 261 BC. He had invaded Kalinga, present day Odisha, for expansion of his territory, but after seeing the destruction caused by the War, he decided to never wage a war again and adopted the path of the Buddha, peace and *Dhamma*. He got a stone railing built all around the tree to protect it from grazing cattle. That stone railing is now preserved in the Archeological Museum at Bodhgaya. A replica has since been erected around the tree which is made of metal.

TREE AT BODH GAYA

All around the temple and the tree the courtyard is cemented and there is a marble parapet where one can sit down comfortably and meditate. There were a lot of people in this area, and yet there was no noise, no dust, no dirt and no disturbance. Everyone was sitting in peace. It was an amazing feeling and left a very soothing and calming effect on me. I felt the centuries disappear and all the commotion, confusion, pollution, stress of my daily life seemed like a thing of some imaginary world. Peace, compassion, calm, and a feeling of kindness, camaraderie and co-existence descended upon me. There was enough space under the all encompassing tree for everyone to sit, relax and meditate.

SUJATA'S STUPA

I felt that in the real world we give importance to so many feelings which are really very unimportant in hind sight. We allow anger, hurt, stress, guilt, rat race, competition and envy to rule our lives.

Perhaps following the eight fold path shown by Buddha would be a path which would make life simpler and happier for everyone. I know this formula sounds very simple, but then one must remember that Buddhism was never meant to be a religion, it only taught us the correct way of living.

CONCEPTUALISATION OF THE COMPLETE ASHOK CHAKRA

4

SARNATH

After attaining enlightenment at Gaya, Siddharth who had now become the Buddha, or the Enlightened One, looked for the other five meditators led by Kaundinya who had been with him wandering from place to place in search of knowledge.

All these people had deserted Siddharth as soon as he had partaken of the *Kheer* that Sujata had brought as an offering for the *Vriksh Devata*. They thought that by leaving extreme penance which they believed was the only way to seek truth, knowledge and salvation, Siddharth had strayed from the path of asceticism. Buddha came to know that these five ascetics had gone towards Varanasi.

He reached Sarnath which in those days was called Isipatana. Sarnath is very close to the Eternal City of Varanasi. "Eternual", because it has been continuously occupied for the last 3000 years. This city is at the confluence of the River Varuna and River Assi with the mighty River Ganga.

Sarnath became the first place to receive the Doctrine or Philosophy of the great thinker Buddha.

Today there are ruins in Sarnath which speak about the places where Buddha meditated, gave his discourse and shared his thoughts which changed the way of life and thoughts with the "Wheel of Change".

There were many rituals, beliefs, practices prevalent in the way that people lived in those days. Buddha introduced the concept of rational thought, the art of questioning, the doctrine of righteousness and right thoughts for improving life.

His most important teaching has been for everyone to reason out and never accept anything blindly without question. He made people realise that blind faith was not acceptable, that living a life of penance and guilt was not correct.

In this life one should follow the correct path which one can decide according to one's reasoning. "Reason, think and decide" these were radical thoughts which lifted a person away from the belief of blind faith and an attitude of reconciliation and acceptance without question. His was a revolutionary idea as he gave each person the right to think and not be a follower of someone else's thinking.

Buddha used simple ways, examples and parables to explain to people his doctrine. It is said that once he asked his followers what would they do if their house was on fire. Would they:
(1) Find the cause of the fire?
(2) Pray for the safety of their life and their possessions?

(3) Make a list of what they were about to lose?

(4) Plan a new house?

The answer was that no one would think of these alternatives. The person whose house was on fire would take immediate and decisive action to put out the fire with his clear and practical thought. There would be no sacrament, no scripture or saviour or ritual to which he would turn.

After about three hundred years of this visit of Buddha to Sarnath, the Great Emperor Ashoka of Magadh spread the philosophy of Buddha far and wide in India as well as in South East Asia. He visited all the places in India associated with Buddha and built huge pillars of *Chunar* Stone, with inscriptions giving information of the importance of the place. This way he recorded history on stone for posterity. The etching was in the script of those days which was *Brahmi*.

These pillars are now known as Ashoka Pillars. In a lot of places all over India we can find these pillars, as they were erected throughout the territory over which the Mauryan Empire was spread. The

Mauryan Empire in those days encompassed almost the entire length and breadth of the Indian sub-continent.

Ashoka also got 84,000 stupas made over the relics of the Buddha all over his empire. When I visited Sarnath, I found two stupas built on two important sites connected with the Buddha. One is the Dhamek stupa, the other is the Chaukhandi stupa.

CHAUKHANDI STUPA

The Chaukhandi stupa is located at the place where Buddha met Kaundinya and the four other ascetics for the first time after becoming enlightened.

Dhamek stupa is the place where Buddha gave his first discourse to these five ascetics. In a straight line from the Dhamek Stupa towards the south are the ruins of another stupa which is called Dharmarajika Stupa.

DHARMARAJIKA STUPA

This stupa was dismantled in 1794 by Jagat Singh, a Dewan of the Rajah of Banaras, who used the stones and bricks from the Stupa to build his palace, without realising what he was destroying.

Dhamek stupa is a very prominent stupa, and there are beautiful designs on its exteriors. As this was the place where Buddha gave his first discourse the place is worshipped by Buddhists who come from all over the world

MULA-GANDHA KUTI

In the same complex is situated the "*Mula-gandha Kuti*", which was the place where Buddha is said to have meditated for three months. When Siddharth got enlightened at Gaya, it was the month of *Vaishakha*, and by the time he reached Sarnath which is about 260 km. away from Gaya, it was the season of the monsoon, as Buddha performed the journey on foot. As the monsoon had set in, Buddha had to stay at Sarnath for *varshawaas.* The *Mula-gandha Kuti* had three doors. Outside the southern door was the Ashoka pillar made of

Chunar stone. Out of all the Ashoka pillars found in India this pillar is the most beautiful one.

PINNACLE OF ASHOKA PILLAR (ACTUAL EXCAVATION PICTURE)

On its pinnacle was a capital with four lions facing four directions. Below this capital of lions, there are sculptures of an elephant, a horse, a bull and a lion separated by four spoked wheels. Each wheel had twenty four spokes.

The entire Capital sits above an inverted lotus. On top of these four seated lions was a wheel with thirty two spokes. This wheel rested on the shoulders of the lions. Sadly, in the thirteenth century this pillar was broken by invaders.

The Capital is now kept in the Sarnath Museum while the broken pieces of the Pillar have been kept in a glass enclosure at its original place. This capital was adopted as the Emblem of the Government of India when the Constitution of India was adopted on 26th January 1950, and India became a Republic after attaining Independence from British Rule in 1947. The wheel with thirty two spokes was broken in many pieces and does not form part of the Emblem. The wheels with twenty four spokes which forms part of the base of the capital, is the wheel at the center of the National flag of India.

The first discourse of Buddha was about *Dharma Chakra Parivartan*. *Dharma Chakra Parivartan* means "Setting in motion the wheel of the *Dhamma* for change".

Therefore, these wheels with spokes speak about the wheel that Buddha set in motion. A wheel as we all know moves, it does not remain fixed. This is the basic philosophy of Buddhism which speaks of movement as against fixed dogmas and beliefs.

> Buddha defined four truths, which are now called Noble Truths: -
> 1 There is the truth of *dukkha* or suufering.
> 2. There is the truth of there being a reason for the *dukkha* or origin for the suffering. It could be due to craving, ignorance, attachment, or aversion.
> 3. There is the truth that there can be a cessation of *dukkha* or suffering by renunciation, release, letting go of craving.
> 4. There is the truth that there is a path which can be followed for cessation of *dukkha* or suffering. That path is the Ashtang Marg.

The first "*Sangh*" was also established at Sarnath, just as the first discourse of Buddhism was given here. A *sangh* is an organised group of people with a shared aim or interest. Yasa, the son of a rich householder of Varanasi along with his fifty four friends became followers of the Buddha after hearing his discourse. The first *Sangh* was therefore founded with these fifty five and the five ascetics led by Kaundinya.

This *sangh* was of sixty monks who went in various directions to preach the new *dhamma* whereby a new order and doctrine of righteous behaviour was laid. *Dhamma* the word then, did not have religious connotations as it has today. What were the exact words of the Buddha when he explained his philosophy is a matter of conjecture, because the wisdom and teachings of the Buddha were written down many years after his death. Till then all these teachings were passed on verbally by the monks to the followers of Buddhism.

Fa Hien and Hiuen Tsang, Chinese travellers, visited Sarnath in the 5th and 7th centuries AD respectively, and left vivid descriptions of the stupas and monasteries that they saw. It is from their writings that we know about all the monasteries at Sarnath as well as the stupas. The Dhamek Stupa is shaped differently from the other stupas which were simply rounded, whereas this is cylindrical.

When I visited Sarnath I found people from different countries worshipping the Dhamek Stupa. The style of prayer of each group was different. The Burmese filled a lot of small glasses with water and kept them on a small wall. They also lit incense sticks and candles in a small area demarcated for the purpose, in the periphery of the stupa.

WATER FILLED GLASSES

The Japanese had a person sounding a wooden gong, the Koreans and Thais sat quietly and meditated. The ladies from Ladakh kept standing, kneeling and prostrating themselves on the ground. All were facing the stupa.

Chanting, praying and venerating the Buddha or praying at the places connected with the life of Buddha is certainly not what Buddha wanted. Buddha wished for people to think, reason and not follow anyone blindly. Treating Buddha like a God to be worshipped, defeats the philosophy of questioning and reasoning which he propounded.

WORSHIPPERS AT DHAMEK STUPA

Moving on from the Stupa, ruins of the monasteries and the *Mool Gandha Kuti*, I visited the Chaukhandi stupa which is a little away from the Dhamek stupa. This was the place where Buddha found Kaundinya and his followers when he arrived here from

Gaya. It is said that these five ascetics did not get up to greet Buddha when they saw him coming, but as he came closer they all stood up to greet the Buddha. The Chaukhandi Stupa has a large garden around it but I found that there were no people praying or meditating at this place. On top of the stupa in the 16th century AD, Govardhan the son of Raja Todarmal of Agra, built a small structure to commemorate the visit of the Mughal Badshah Humayun to Sarnath.

From the Chaukhandi stupa I went to see the Museum at Sarnath which was constructed in 1905. This was the first museum of the Archeological Survey of India and in keeping with the ethos of the place, was designed like a monastery. The display of artefacts in this museum is splendid. They belong from 3rd century BC to 12th century AD and have been displayed more or less according to the year to which they belong. It is interesting to note that after the eleventh century AD, the statues are mainly of Hindu deities.

The Capital of the Ashoka Pillar of Sarnath is kept at this Museum, and is the first item that one can see as one enters the

Museum. There are a couple of gigantic statues belonging to the 2nd century BC which have also been displayed prominently.

DHAMEK STUPA

A statue of the Buddha belonging to the 5th century AD is a highly prized possession. At the base of this statue are the kneeling figures of Kaundinya and his followers as well as of a woman with a child. It is thought that perhaps this lady had got the statue made. In those day people who could afford it, would get statues made depicting themselves as the devotee of the Buddha.

Just as Varanasi is considered a very important city for pilgrimage by the Hindus, Sarnath too is one of the most important places connected with the followers of Buddhism. Sarnath is the place where Buddha gave the first discourse of his philosophy. This is also the place where the *Sangh* was formulated and from where the philosophy of Buddha started reaching people in all directions.

LUMBINI to KUSHINARA

ASHOKA PILLAR

BASE OF THE ASHOKA CHAKRA FOUND AT SARNATH

BUDDHA 5th CENTURY AD

5

RAJGRIH

After setting up the *Sangh* at Sarnath, Buddha proceeded towards Rajgrih to locate his first gurus, Alara Kalam and Udaka Ramputta with whom he wanted to share his new found knowledge. He was quite disappointed to know that both these teachers had since died. Bimbisar the ruler of Magadha accepted the teachings of Buddha, became a Buddhist and requested Buddha to stay on at Rajgrih.

A large *Venuvan* or Bamboo Grove was given to the Buddha for his stay as well as for the stay of his followers. Buddha met two of his ardent followers Sariputta and Moggalayan at Rajgrih.

WHERE BUDDHA PREACHED

Buddha was a person with a mission, who wanted to spread his teachings far and wide and so he did not want to stay at one place for too long. He went from place to place spreading his teachings. During his lifetime he returned to Rajgrih a number of times and stayed here altogether for twelve years. In those days travelling was not easy. During the monsoons it was not possible to travel as, often the rivers would be flooded and roads would be washed away due to the continuous rain. Buddha would therefore stay at one place during the rainy season which would last for around four months from July to October. This stay was called the "*varshavaas*". Often this *varshavaas* was done at the *Venuvan* at Rajgrih.

Rajgrih, like Rome, is surrounded by hills. Through the ages there has been peace, plenty and prosperity in this area. First came Buddha and then it is said, Mahavira too spent 14 years at Rajgrih, in the 6th century BC.

BIMBISAR'S PRISON

I, in the 21st century following the trail of the Buddha reached Rajgrih from Sarnath. Rajgrih which was once the Capital of a mighty empire called Magadh, is now a small town and is simply known as Rajgir.

In the 6th century BC, Ajatshatru the son of Bimbisar wanted to expand his kingdom, and so he imprisoned his father, wrested power from him and went forth in his quest for expansion.

Bimbisar was imprisoned at the foothills of the Gridhrakoot hill at Rajgrih. Whenever the Buddha was stationed at Rajgrih, he would climb up the hill to preach his sermons to all his followers. Bimbisar would look at the Buddha while he was climbing the hill and watch him preaching. Gridhrakoot hill is the hill where the Shanti Stupa is now located. One has the choice to take the old steps or take the Ropeway to reach the Shanti Stupa

When I reached Rajgir from Gaya, I found a small enclosure, where grooves are formed on the rocky terrain. These grooves may have been formed by the speeding ancient chariot of Krishna, when he came to wage war with Jarasandha during *Mahabharata* time. It is not known when exactly the *Mahabharata* war took place, but most probably it happened around 3000 BC, according to some sources.

It is said in the *Mahabharata* that, Krishna fought with Jarasandha 17 times and in the 18th attack he left the war grounds, that is the reason why Krishna is also called *Ranchhod* or "deserter from war". We saw some writing on the rocks in a script which is called the *Shankh lipi*. This writing has not yet been deciphered, therefore we could not make out what had been written there.

CHARIOT WHEEL GROOVE MARKS

There is an interesting cave at Rajgrih. It is called the "*Swarn Bhandar*" of Bimbisar. The outline of a door is carved on the rock and there is some writing in *Shankh lipi*, which is said to be the mantra to open the door. This cave is supposed to contain treasures of King Bimbisar's empire.

WALL SCULPTURES - BIMBISAR TREASURY

There are nice carvings of the Buddha on the walls, but most of them had been defaced by the Khiljis when they attacked the University of Nalanda as well as Rajgrih, in the 13th century AD. Our earliest international tourists, devotees and scholars Fa Hian and Hiuen Tsang who came from China have written extensively about Rajgrih in their books, from which we learn about the times at Rajgir in those days.

The First Buddhist Council (*sangiti*) was held in the Saptaparni cave, near the

Swarn Bhandar soon after the death of Buddha, under the leadership of Maha Kassapa, along with Upali & Anand, *bhikkus* and devoted followers of the Buddha. Rules and tenets of Buddhism, *vinaya* and *dhamma,* were formulated in this Council and doubts if any were cleared.

BIMBISAR'S TREASURY

It is said that the famous physician Jivaka also lived in Rajgrih. Jivaka had studied at the Takshashila University of North Western India, now in Pakistan. He had treated Buddha when Buddha was attacked by his cousin Devdutt. There was a Jivaka-mara-vana monastery here.

Rajgrih has a stupa made by Ajatshatru. We also find hot sulphur springs here which are said to cure ailments of the skin.

The main mode of transport at Rajgir today is the horse drawn *Tonga*. It is a very pleasant ride on this vehicle as the sound of the hooves of the horse make a mesmerising rhythmic trot. The *tongawalla* narrates his tale about Rajgrih, the majesty of the hills surrounding Rajgrih are visible, and the thought that Buddha spent so many *varshavaas* months here teaching, preaching and enlightening the people of this land, enchants you. The hills, the bamboo groves, the ruins are mute spectators of time having taken its toll.

Buddha who convinced people through reason and persuasion has said that there are a few Universal Truths in the world. The first is "*Aniccha*" or impermanence, which means that the world is constantly changing, nothing is permanent, life itself is mortal.

6

NALANDA

Nalanda is a small town close to Rajgrih in Bihar. From the 5th century AD to 12th century AD there was a very famous University at Nalanda. The University flourished under the rule of the Gupta Empire and later under King Harsha-vardhana, the Emperor of Kannauj (606-648 AD). Harsha remitted the revenues of nearly one hundred villages for the maintenance of the University therefore, no fees were charged from the students.

During the medieval times the Pala Kings of Bengal and Bihar were the patrons of this University. The Palas also established new monasteries at Vikramashila, Somapura, Odantapuri and Jagaddala in eastern part of India. Hiuen Tsang, a scholar of China came to study in Nalanda in 630 AD. He carried Buddhist literature with him back to China and a number of these books are now kept in the city of Xian in the Shaanxi Province. The Great Wild Goose Pagoda was constructed in 652 AD to house the translations of Buddhist *Suttas* brought back by Hiuen Tsang.

PEACEFUL SURROUNDINGS

A University is "Studium Generale" which means it is a place where students from everywhere are welcome, where not only Arts but at least one of the higher faculties of Theology, law or medicine is taught and where teaching is done by Masters. This description fits Nalanda as there was an assemblage of strangers from all parts of the world in one spot with teachers and students for every department of knowledge.

A MONASTERY - NALANDA

At Nalanda there were international students who came to study from Tibet, China, Korea and Central Asia. Pilgrim monks who came to study at this University wrote about this place and therefore our knowledge about the place comes from those writings. It is said that in the 13th century, Bakhtiar Khilji ransacked and destroyed the University. The books in the Library were also set on fire. The Library was huge and had a massive collection of books, so the fire had raged continuously for three months.

Even today one can see burnt brick walls which speak volumes about this sad act of arson. Today in the 21st century we are very proud of our heritage, our *parampara*, our knowledge, our ancient glory, wisdom, development of art, science, *niti* and advancement in astronomy, mathematics, dance and music. All these and more were taught at our great centers of learning in olden times, of which the best known are Takshashila, Nalanda and Vikramshila.

SARIPUTTA'S STUPA

A few famous teachers of Takshashila were Chanakya, a learned Economist as well as Philosopher, Vishnu Sharma who wrote the Pancha-Tantra, Charaka the Physician, Panini the Grammar Exponent and Jivaka, the Physician of the Buddha. A famous alumni of Takshashila was Chandragupta Maurya, who established the Mauryan Empire of Magadh and was the grandfather of Ashoka the Great.

Takshashila was in existence since 8th century BC, and continued to attract students from around the old world until the destruction of the University in the 5th century AD by the Huns. Students came here from Babylon, Greece, Syria, Arabia, Phoenicia, China, Magadha, Kashi and Kosala.

In spite of the long and arduous journey they had to undergo, the excellence of the learned teachers brought students from all over. The teachers were recognized as authorities in their respective subjects. There were about 68 different streams of discipline and about 10,500 students would be studying there at any one time.

This University's primary concern was not with elementary, but with higher education. Generally, a student entered Takshashila at the age of sixteen. When Alexander attacked India in the 4th century BC, he took back with him a number of scholars from here. Therefore, we find that a lot of myths, and stories are quite similar between Greece, Syria and India.

A MONASTERY

Vikramshila is the lesser known University, which is located in Bihar near Bhagalpur. It came into existence after the Nalanda University went into its decline. In the first 300 years of its existence, Nalanda flourished with liberal cultural traditions but from 9th century onwards its decline set in as *Tantricism* became more pronounced. Yijing

(673-695 AD) a Chinese Buddhist scholar says that when he was at Nalanda there were 300 rooms and 8 colleges, and matters of discussion and administration required an assembly. Consensus had to be arrived at by all the monks at the assembly. Even those resident monks who were absent from the Assembly at that particular time would have to give their consensus later.

My journey on the path traversed by the great Buddha took me from Rajgrih to Nalanda. The gate to this center of learning, education and wisdom was quite small. But as soon as I went inside, it was like entering a different world, where there was no noise, no sound, nothing but bricks, and ruins which spoke of the amazing brilliance of this place. It was as if I had entered from a tunnel into a space filled with light. One saw ruins of monasteries, temples and stupas lined up in neat rows.

According to folklore, a person seeking admission to Nalanda University was first interviewed by the *dwarpal* or the doorman of the University. Religion, logic, metaphysics and many more disciplines were taught here. Students came from Korea,

Japan, Iran, Indonesia and China, besides Magadh, Kosala and Kashi.

Each Monastery was a complete unit by itself. There were rooms for students and each room had a built in bed and a shelf for keeping books. Two students would share a room. In each Monastery there was a common kitchen, a well, and a raised platform for the teacher to sit and give his discourse. There would be no forced learning, it was the student whose desire to learn was paramount.

A BED & BOOKSHELF

Nalanda is the place from where knowledge spread. It encouraged a quest for learning, free and radical thinking, where learning was for betterment and improvement of the self. There were no certificates awarded, there were no jobs guaranteed, there was no money at the end of the knowledge gates. It was emancipation, enlightenment, and development of the self. Learning was at its best, the thirst and quest for knowledge was the essence of existence.

Knowledge, freedom from blind faith and eventual enlightenment can only be achieved when we open our minds, question, discuss and then get convinced. Thirst for knowledge can only be quenched by questioning. This was what Buddha had taught.

Nalanda did not exist at the time of the Buddha, but was a center of learning for the thoughts of the Buddha.

Varsha Uke Nagpal

7

VAISHALI

There were 16 confederacies in North India at the time of the Buddha. One of the bigger confederacy in those days was the Vajji Mahajanapada which had its capital at Vaishali. This city was located in the *terai* region with plenty of river water which brought a lot of silt with it, therefore this fertile land was very prosperous. When there is plenty of food and all basic needs are met, then human race progresses, flourishes and development takes place in other aspects of life, like art, culture and philosophy.

In olden times King Vishal ruled over Vaishali. There is a pond near the palace of King Vishal where the *Abhishek* or anointment of the King was done every year. Vaishali was a flourishing City State with a great cultural heritage.

Ajatshatru the King of Magadh wanted to conquer Vaishali but had repeatedly been unsuccessful. Ajatshatru therefore asked Buddha what made Vaishali invincible. He was told by the Buddha that the Vajji clan of Vaishali had certain traits which gave them an edge over others:

> (1) They were punctual at their meetings, and had frequent public assemblies.
> (2) They were disciplined, and acted in concord at their meetings and assemblies
> (3) They respected, honoured and held in esteem their elders and women.
> (4) They did not forcefully marry off their daughters and acted in accordance with Vajjian law.
> (5) They gave protection to the *Arhats* (one who is worthy.)

(6) They had *Chaityas* inside the town, which were maintained well.

Buddha thought that these practices were very good and when he organised the *Bhikku Sangh* he introduced the patterns of Vaishali democracy in it.

There was a practice at Vaishali, that the most beautiful girl of the region was made the *nagar-vadhu* or Bride of the City. The most beautiful girl would be chosen, trained in the art of music and dance, and would be the courtesan who would have to be the bride of anyone who could pay her price. Amrapali was one such *nagar-vadhu*. It is said that this tradition was started by King Manudev of the Lichchavi clan as he wished to possess Amrapali, but Amrapali wanted to marry someone else. By starting this practice Manudev deprived Amrapali the freedom of marrying the person of her choice.

At the time of the Buddha, only men were allowed to become monks and live in monasteries. Maha Prajapati Gautami, the step mother of Siddharth who had brought him up, requested Buddha to allow women to join the *Sangh*, so that they would also get an opportunity to follow the teachings as well as propagate and preach the philosophy of the Buddha.

WOMEN'S MONASTERY

Ananda a follower as well as a cousin of Buddha also took up this issue and persuaded Buddha to allow women to join the *Sangh*. This revolutionary step of granting equality to women was therefore taken at Vaishali. Amrapali the *nagar-vadhu*, also became a disciple of the Buddha, renounced the world and joined the *Bhikkuni Sangh.* The village of Ambada Chowk near present day Vaishali is the place where Amrapali lived around 600 BC. It is said that there is a Girls School at the spot where Amrapali once lived.

ASHOK STAMBH AT VAISHALI

Buddha would often come to Vaishali to preach and also spent many *varshavaas* seasons here. A number of *Vinaya* rules were formulated during the *varshavaas* of Buddha at Vaishali.

The Second Buddhist Council (*sangiti*) was held at Vaishali after about one hundred years of the death of Buddha, where certain rules to be followed by the *bhikkus* were discussed.

At the age of 80, Buddha gave his last discourse and sermon here and declared to the assembled people that he was departing from Vaishali and would soon be leaving the world forever. The people of Vaishali were very upset at this disclosure and kept following him on his journey away from Vaishali. They refused to go back to their city and wanted to keep following Buddha on his last journey.

Breathing in the air of Vaishali, walking on the road taken by the Great Teacher, I in the 21st century, could visualize the surge of humanity grieving at the imminent death of their beloved Teacher. The thought that they would never see him or hear him again was surely the ultimate grief.

The Buddha had said, "The whole secret of existence is to have no fear. Never fear what will become of you, depend on no one. Only the moment you reject all help, you are free."

STUPA OPENED BY ASHOKA

When I was travelling to Vaishali, on the path that Gautama the Buddha walked 2600 years ago, while crossing the mighty Ganga, I looked at the vast expanse of water with reverence as it had allowed such a great civilization to flourish here. Perhaps that is the reason why this humongous Ganga is considered sacred. So many rivers have already flown into the Ganga by this time that all the soil, and culture seems to have converged together.

There is a Stupa near the *Abhishek* tank at Vaishali where the relics of the Buddha were preserved after his death. This Stupa was opened by Ashoka in the 3rd century BC, the Relics were removed and smaller portions were distributed all over India. 84,000 Stupas were built over these distributed relics by Ashoka.

ANANDA'S STUPA

Just outside the town of Vaishali is another stupa where the relics of Anand the most favourite *shishya* of Buddha are preserved. There are also the ruins of a Swastika shaped monastery which was supposed to be the monastery of women headed by Prajapati Gautami. An Ashoka

Pillar can also be seen here with a single sitting lion at the pinnacle of the pillar.

Time has taken its toll and today Vaishali is just a bit bigger than a small town of rural India. The might, beauty and glory that it once possessed has vanished. What once was a much coveted City and where Buddha stayed and preached for many years, no longer wields the power it did once upon a time.

Alas! Vaishali the capital of the invincible Republic of the Vajjians, the place where Buddha granted equal opportunity to women, the place where he announced his impending death and where he gave his last sermon has lost its glory. It is now a forgotten town.

Varsha Uke Nagpal

8

KESARIYA

Kesariya in the times of the Buddha was called Kessaputta. It falls on the route that Buddha took on his journey from Rajgrih to Kushinara and Nepal. This place was ruled by Kalamas and later by the Kosalas. It is said that the first teacher of Siddharth at Rajgrih, Alara Kalam belonged to Kessaputta.

This place is 55 kilometres north of Vaishali. When Buddha declared at Vaishali that he was leaving Vaishali forever, the people of Vaishali were heart broken and left their homes and followed Buddha.

At Kesariya, Buddha told the people of Vaishali to return to their homes. He gave them his *bhiksha patra* as a token of remembrance. He also told them not to grieve for him. This *bhiksha patra* was kept first at Kesariya and later moved to Vaishali where it was venerated. In the 2nd century AD, King Kanishka of Kushan dynasty of Afghanistan, who was also a Buddhist, invaded Vaishali and took away the *Bhiksha Patra* with him to his capital Peshawar. It is now kept in Kabul, Afghanistan.

This is the place where Buddha gave his discourse called Kessaputtiya *Sutta* also called the Kalama *Sutta*. It was here that Buddha is supposed to have given his discourse where he said that his followers must analyse his teachings thoroughly before accepting them, "*Atta Deep Bhava*". This was granting the people freedom of thought.

Buddha advised the people of Kessaputta to use solid logical reasoning and the dialectic principles for enquiry to seek truth, wisdom and knowledge. These teachings encouraged people to not accept any teachings or dogmas blindly. It propagated questioning and reasoning. It opposed blind faith. A stupa was made at the place where Buddha gave this sermon. This Stupa was seen by Hiuen Tsang and Fa Hien too, and was described in their writings. It was built sometime between 200 AD and 750 AD. The Stupa is said to be the largest stupa in the world. It has five levels and each level differs in shape. On every level there are niches where statues of Buddha were kept.

KESARIYA STUPA

Over a period of time this stupa got quite dilapidated and there was over growth of vegetation over it. It was lost to the world as it looked like a mound until it was discovered in 1958 by the Archeological Survey of India. Even today only half of the Stupa has been excavated and one can see the beauty of the carvings. The remaining half still looks like a hillock with trees and overgrowth. The work of excavation is going on at a slow and steady pace.

NICHES WITH STATUES

When I reached Kesariya, I was amazed to see the size of the Stupa. It was very big and even in its dilapidated state looked beautiful. After walking around, when we were leaving, the guard at the gate asked us if we had seen the statues of the Buddha. As we had not seen them, he told us to go back and look again from a little distance from a particular spot, at an angle. We went back and then could see a number of statues in niches. Sadly, all of them had been defaced and a number of them had been smashed by the Khiljis when they came to this area in the 13th century. I wonder what point is proved when ancient magnificence is destroyed. History remains history even if work of art pertaining to that period is destroyed.

Kesariya gave us the first teacher of Siddharth, Alara Kalam and was the place where the Sermon of "*Atta Deep Bhava*" was given.

9

SHRAWASTI

During the 6th century BC, at the time of the Buddha, Shrawasti located at the foothills of the Himalayas, near the river Rapti, was the capital of the Kosala Kingdom. It was then called Shavathhi and the River Rapti was then called Achiravati. The Buddha spent 24 monsoon months (*varshavaas*) at Shrawasti. Kapilvastu and Devdaha were vassals of the Kosala Kingdom and Raja Prasenjit or Pasenadi was the King of Kosala then. Merchants would move around neighbouring places in connection with their business. The road from Rajgrih of the Magadha Kingdom to Shrawasti of the Kosala Kingdom passed through Vaishali. It is said that a prosperous *Shreshti* named Sudatta of Shrawasti also called "*Anath Pindika*" because of his generosity to orphans had visited Rajgriha where he heard the discourse of Buddha. He wanted to invite Buddha to Shrawasti and therefore wanted to buy a large garden for Buddha's stay and to construct a Vihara for his followers.

BUDDHA PREACHED HERE

The garden that he selected was very huge and was owned by Prince Jeta, who did not wish to part with the garden. Prince Jeta, therefore, told Sudatta that if he covered the garden with gold coins the garden would be given to him. It is said that Sudatta covered the place with 108 million gold pieces and donated the place for use of the Buddha. Today this is the place where a number of ruins of viharas and temples have been found. It is now called Sahet. Buddha spent twenty four *varshavaas* at Shrawasti.

BUDDHA MEDITATED HERE

When I visited Shrawasti following the path of the Buddha, I found that the place is maintained beautifully. The garden is very huge and spread out. There were many monasteries here once upon a time which are now in ruins, the place where Buddha usually sat and meditated as well as the strip where he would take a walk are well preserved. There is an *Anandakuti* and a *Gandha kuti* here. *Anandakuti* is the place where Bhikku Ananda stayed at the time of the Buddha. Ananda was a close associate of the Buddha and had been with him till the time of the death of Buddha. Ananda was the son of King Shudhodhan's brother and therefore was a cousin of Buddha. There is an Ananda *Bodhi* tree at Sahet which is venerated. The sapling was brought here from Bodhgaya by Ananda.

The first woman disciple of Buddha also belonged to Shrawasti. She was Vishakha, who was the daughter of Dhananjaya and Sumana Devi who originally belonged to Magadh, which was a prosperous place where there were a number of *shreshtis* or merchants. Dhananjaya shifted to Shrawasti in search of better business opportunities. Vishakha was married to Punnavaddhana the son of Migara, a rich but miserly merchant of Shrawasti. Vishakha built the Pubbarama Monastery, where Buddha spent six years of *varshavaas*. She was a wise lady and devoted to the Buddha.

LUMBINI to KUSHINARA

After sitting inside the ruin of the little area where Buddha used to meditate, I learnt that peace and forgiveness is the biggest virtue of all times.

ANGULIMALA'S PRISON

From Sahet we went to a place called Mahet where there are two stupas called the "*pakki kuti*" and the "*kacchi kuti*" The *kacchi kuti* is the stupa of Anath pindika and the *pakki kuti* is the jail of *Angulimala*.

Angulimala it is said had studied at Takshashila, but had later become a dacoit who waylaid travellers and cut off their little finger and put a garland of the cut fingers around his neck. After meeting the Buddha, he was reformed and gave up this crime. The *pakki kuti* mound or Stupa is over Angulimala's jail.

King Prasenjit or Pasenadi as he was then called built the Rajakarama Monastery.

Pasenadi had also studied at Takshshila. As both Kosala and Magadh were large empires, there were a lot of intermarriages between the royal families. King Pasenadi was married to a princess of Magadh, and his own sister Devi was married to King Bimbisar of Magadh. Pasenadi also wanted to marry a daughter of the Shakya clan of Kapilvastu, as he wanted to build a relationship with Buddha. The Shakyas considered themselves superior, therefore, did not want to fix alliance with their own princess. Mahanama an cousin of Buddha had a daughter with a slave girl and the Shakyas cleverly offered this girl's hand to Pasenadi. Not knowing these details, Pasenadi married Vasabhakhatiya and had a daughter named Vajira, who was later married to Ajatshatru of Magadh.

Pasenadi was very devoted to the Buddha but wondered how Buddha had become enlightened at such a young age. At this the Buddha had told him not to doubt a noble warrior, a serpent, fire and a bhikku, because an enraged warrior may cause harm, the bite of a serpent may kill, a small fire may turn into an inferno and a young bhikku could also be enlightened.

Near these ruins and stupas of Sahet and Mahet, there are beautiful temples built by the Srilankan, Chinese, Myanmarese and Thais. Close by is a huge bell donated by the Japanese.

SRILANKAN PILGRIMS

Shrawasti was a very fertile and developed place at the time of Buddha. It was quite populated and was the capital of the Kosala Kingdom. There were business as well as family links between the people of Kosala, Magadh, and Kaushambi in the south, therefore roads were well developed.

LUMBINI to KUSHINARA

Shrawasti was the place where Buddha spent maximum number of varshawaas and monastic life. He came to Shrawasti from Rajgriha at the invitation of *Anath pindika*. His followers who are known to this day were Vishakha, Prasenjit, Angulimaal and of course *Anath pindika*.

Varsha Uke Nagpal

10

KAUSHAMBI

While Buddha was at Shrawasti, a *Shreshti* of Kaushambi heard his discourse and invited him to visit Kaushambi. Kaushambi was the capital of the Vatsa *Ganarajya*, which was located near the river Yamuna and present day Allahabad. It was a very prosperous city where a number of merchants lived, as it was an entreport of goods and people from north, west and south, as people travelled from Magadh to Shrawasti, Avanti and in other directions. Business and trade was well developed and trade Guilds existed. Coins and seals bearing the name of Kaushambi have been found belonging to the 3rd century BC. One of the more well known guilds of Kaushambi was a perfumers guild, as coins have been discovered here named *"Gandhikanama"*.

KAUSHAMBI - A PLANNED CITY

Kaushambi was a fortified town and had three gates facing the east, west and north with moats all around. The Yamuna river flanked the town on the south side. It was a well developed and planned town as there were dwelling units laid out in straight lines.

LUMBINI to KUSHINARA

At the time of the Buddha in the 6th century BC, Udayan was the ruler of the Vatsa *Ganarajya*, and he was a follower of the Buddha. Buddha visited Kaushambi in the sixth and ninth year after attaining enlightenment.

RUINS OF A MONASTERY

There were four Monasteries at Kaushambi. One was Ghositarama, Kukkuta rama, Pavarika Ambavana and Badarika. These monasteries were established by the rich merchants named Ghosita, Kukkuta, Pavarika and Badrika. Whenever Buddha visited Kaushambi he would stay at one of these monasteries. A number of *Suttas* of the Buddha were formulated at Kaushambi.

The first known dispute in the *Sangh* occurred at Kaushambi while the Buddha was in town. Buddha tried to intervene but the monks asked him to allow them to sort out their matter. Buddha left the monastery and went back to Shrawasti. Later the monks realised their mistake and apologised to the Buddha.

GHOSITARAMA MONASTRY

When I visited Kaushambi, I found the ruins were spread in a vast area, these were of dwelling houses. The walls were in a straight line and the dwelling units seemed to have a common pattern.

ASHOKA PILLAR

Ashoka had visited this place and got an Ashoka Pillar built here. This pillar is now in quite a damaged state. At the time when Ashoka visited Kaushambi the monasteries were flourishing. Yet it appears that the

Sanghs were not very peaceful and disputes were rising amongst the resident monks.

This becomes evident from the edict on the Ashoka pillar found here which states:-

"The King instructs the officials of Kaushambi as follows: -
The way of the *Sangh* must not be abandoned, who so ever shall break the unity of *Sangh*, whether monk or nun from this time forth, shall be compelled to wear white garments, and to dwell in a place outside the *Sangh*."

The Ghositarama monastery was a little away from the ruins of the main residential area. I found that the town of Kaushambi was built at a higher level. The reason could be to save themselves from flood waters of the River Yamuna.

Looking at the ruins of Kaushambi it is impossible to imagine the glory it once enjoyed. It is even more difficult to imagine that this was a busy commercial place through which many merchants passed on their way from Avanti, Varanasi, Magadh or Shrawasti. All the grandeur, wealth and beauty of the place has been ravaged with time. The ruins located at a higher level stand mute, desolate and isolated. I found young boys of the neighbouring villages grazing their goats on what once was a place filled with buildings, business places, guilds and people.

Kaushambi incidentally also finds mention in the *Mahabharata*, which was a story about a war which took place around 3000 B.C.

Fa Hien had visited this place, and had found that it was a flourishing and well inhabited town. Today Kaushambi is a place with nothing but ruins of ancient dwelling units as well as monasteries and a broken Ashoka Pillar.

11

KUSHINARA

In 483 BC, Buddha chose Kushinara now called Kushinagar as the last place that he would live in. He announced at Vaishali that he was leaving Vaishali for ever, then at Kesariya he gave his begging bowl to the people of Vaishali and asked them to go back to their own town and not grieve for him. From Kesariya he moved further northwards until he reached Kushinara which is about 124 kilometers from Kesariya.

Kushinagar is in present day UP near the river Hiranyavati. The place is not far from the Nepal border and also Kapilvastu to which place Siddharth belonged. During the days of the Buddha, the Mallas were the rulers here, and this place was one of the sixteen *ganarajyas* of 6th century BC.

PLACE WHERE BUDDHA DIED

After arriving at Kushinara, the condition of Buddha deteriorated. Seeing this Ananda was very unhappy. Buddha told Ananda, "Don't grieve Ananda. The nature of things dictates that we must leave those dear to us. Everything born contains its own cessation. I too Ananda, am grown old, and full of years, my journey is drawing to its close. I am turning 80 years of age, and just as a worn out cart can only with much additional care be made to move along, so too the body of the Buddha can only be kept going with much additional care."

The compassionate Buddha on his death bed told the assembled people not to blame Cunda who had served Buddha his last meal, after which he had fallen ill. Doing so he left us a message that compassion and forgiveness are great virtues.

KUSHINARA

Before his death he asked all the assembled bhikkus if they had any doubts about the *Dhamma* or the *Sangh*. They were all invited to get their doubts cleared. Buddha asked them this question three times. He told them that he had taught them everything he knew and that, in future the teachings themselves should be their primary refuge and source of direction. To gain liberation from suffering, they must integrate the teachings into themselves and not depend on any leader or community to save them. When no one had any doubts, Buddha spoke his last words, which were, "Listen, bhikkus, I say this, all conditioned things are subject to decay, strive with diligence for your liberation."

RAMABHAR STUPA

After the death of the Buddha, he was cremated on the bank of the River Hiranyavati. A stupa was later built over the place. It is now called the Ramabhar Stupa. Earlier it was called Mukut Bandhana Chaitya.

Buddha was a much loved person who gave a great philosophy to mankind. After his cremation there were many claimants to his ashes as everyone claimed that he belonged to them. The ashes were therefore collected and divided into eight portions. The spot where the ashes were divided is also maintained well today. The ashes were then given to (1) Ajatshatru of Magadh, (2) Licchavis of Vaishali, (3) Shakyas of Kapilvastu to which clan he belonged, (4) Koliyas of Ramagama clan to which his mother Mahamaya and wife Yashodhara belonged, (5) Buli of Allakappa, (6) Mallas of Kushinara, (7) Mallas of Pava and the (8) Vethadipa Brahman.

All of them took the ashes and built stupas over the ashes. In the 3rd century BC, Emperor Ashoka opened up a few stupas and divided the relics into smaller portions. He got 84,000 stupas built all over India over these relics, thus spreading the message of the Buddha and his relics all over the land that he ruled.

Siddharth born in a princely family of Northern India then and Nepal now, became a great teacher of the whole world. He left a great legacy for humankind. In spite of the fact that he lived 2600 years ago, his thoughts, his philosophy, continue to live on. His philosophy teaches us to be rational and better human beings. It teaches us to think for ourselves. He gave us a message of peace, compassion, kindness and equality.

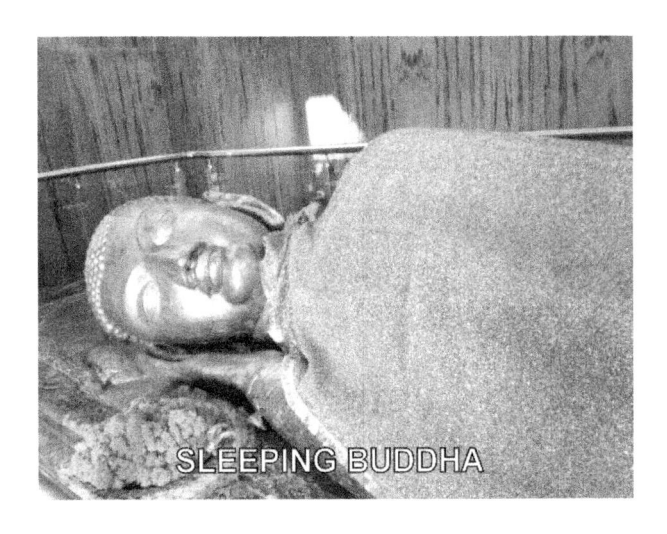

SLEEPING BUDDHA

As I, in the 21st century entered the small town of Kushinara now called Kushinagar, the first thing I saw was the *Parinirvana* Temple. This temple is built on the spot where Buddha died. In 1956, this temple was built by the Government of India as part of the commemoration of the 2500th

LUMBINI to KUSHINARA

year of the *Mahaparinirvana* of this great man.

There is a beautiful statue of the reclining Buddha lying on his right side with his head to the north and facing the west. The statue is 6.1 meter long and is made of *Chunar* stone. This statue is a very old one and belongs to the 5th century AD.

I then went to see the Ramabhar Stupa. This is the spot where Buddha was cremated. Close by is the spot where the ashes of the Buddha were distributed amongst the claimants.

Visiting these places had a profound impact on me, made me think about death, which is the culmination of the journey of human life.

What lives on after death is the memory of the person, long after he is dead.

There are so many questions that surfaced in my mind:-

- How many people's life did I touch?

- What legacy will I leave?

- What difference did I make to the world?

- Will I leave it a better place?

- Did I bring a smile on the face of the people who mattered to me?

- Has my life been lived well?

The eighty year journey of Siddharth which began in Lumbini ended in Kushinara. Both the places are not too far away from each other geographically, but the message of the Buddha, the light that he gave us, the path that he showed us have spread far and wide all over the world.

12

SANCHI

Sanchi is a place which was not visited by Buddha. Buddha in his entire life time remained within the region which is now in Nepal, Bihar and in the east as well as north of UP.

Ashoka was the Emperor of Magadh in 3rd century BC, and had lived in Vidisha in present day Madhya Pradesh as Governor when his father Bindusar was King of Magadh. Ashoka married Devi, the daughter of a merchant of Vidisha. After becoming the Emperor of Magadh and expanding his empire Ashoka became a Buddhist. Then he began spreading the philosophy of Buddha and started building Ashoka Pillars and stupas at places closely connected with the life of Buddha. He also left a number of stone edicts all over his empire which spoke about Buddhism.

SANCHI STUPA

Although Buddha had not visited Sanchi, Ashoka chose a small hillock near Vidisha where he had governed earlier in his life and built a Stupa. Sanchi was in those days called Kakanaya. The stupa that Ashoka built was a low brick structure and was half the diameter of what it presently is.

GATES & PINNACLE

The Sungas who were the next dynasty after the Mauryans, enlarged the Stupa, covered it with stones and placed an umbrella on the top enhancing the beauty of the stupa. They also got a balustrade made around it. The four gates at the Sanchi Stupa were added in the 1st century AD by the Satvahanas. Each gate has beautiful sculptures narrating the story of the Buddha. There are sculptures of women on the pillars with hair styles which are quite akin to what we have now.

FEMALE FORMS ON GATES

There are carvings on the gates of various animals like the horse, elephant, peacock, goat and lions.

There are a few more stupas in the vicinity of the main Stupa. One of them was built on the relics of Moggalayan, a disciple of Gautam Buddha.

There are the ruins of a monastery also in this place where Mahendra and Sanghamitra the children of Emperor Ashoka preached Buddhism before they set out to spread the message of Buddhism to Srilanka and other far eastern countries of Asia.

SCULPTURES ON THE GATE

Vidisha is the place where Ashoka lived, built the Sanchi Stupa and monasteries. Sanchi Stupa is the most beautiful stupa as its gates and statues add to the beauty of the stupa. Although Buddha never came here, yet Sanchi is a part of the Buddhist Circuit.

When I visited the stupa I was quite fascinated by the beautiful gates. The work of depiction of the life of Buddha on the gates was often commissioned by people who could afford to pay for the work. Their names are also etched on the panel which they may have requisitioned.

It is amazing to note that all those places where major Kingdoms flourished with developed art and architecture, have all become small little towns with nothing but ruins which tell us about their past glory.

13

PATALIPUTRA

At the time of the Buddha, Pataliputra had just been made the capital of the Magadh empire by Ajatshatru in 490 BC. He shifted his base from Rajgrih to Pataliputra on the banks of the River Ganga as he wanted to conquer Vaishali which was another very important *Ganarajya* in those days, and was located to the north of Pataliputra.

In 322 BC, the Nandas ruled from Pataliputra. They were the first non-

kshatriya rulers at that time. They had vast armies and had a vast empire. They were the rulers when Alexander had invaded India, but as the Macedonians led by him went back without crossing the Indus river, the Nanda army could not prove their might. They had imposed heavy taxes and it is said that they had become very tyrannical, therefore Chanakya, a *brahmin*, became instrumental in the downfall of the Nanda empire by setting up the Maurya Empire with its first King being Chandragupta Maurya who was the son of a *kshatriya* father and *shudra* mother. Chandragupta Maurya spread his kingdom further south beyond the Vindhyachal range of mountains. He became the Emperor of territories from Hindukush mountains in present day Afghanistan to areas which are now in Bangladesh. It covered the entire sub-continent except some parts of present day Tamilnadu, Kerala and Odisha. The Magadh Empire became one of the largest empires in the world at that time. Ashoka was Chandragupta Maurya's grandson who adopted the path of the Buddha, almost 300 years after the death of the Buddha.

When Ashoka became King, there were a few stupas built over the relics of the

LUMBINI to KUSHINARA

Buddha in a limited area confined to Bihar, and the Buddhist philosophy too had not reached far and wide. Ashoka therefore visited all the places connected with the life and times of the Buddha and got Ashoka pillars made of *Chunar* stone erected in these important places. *Chunar* stone was the local stone available near Pataliputra.

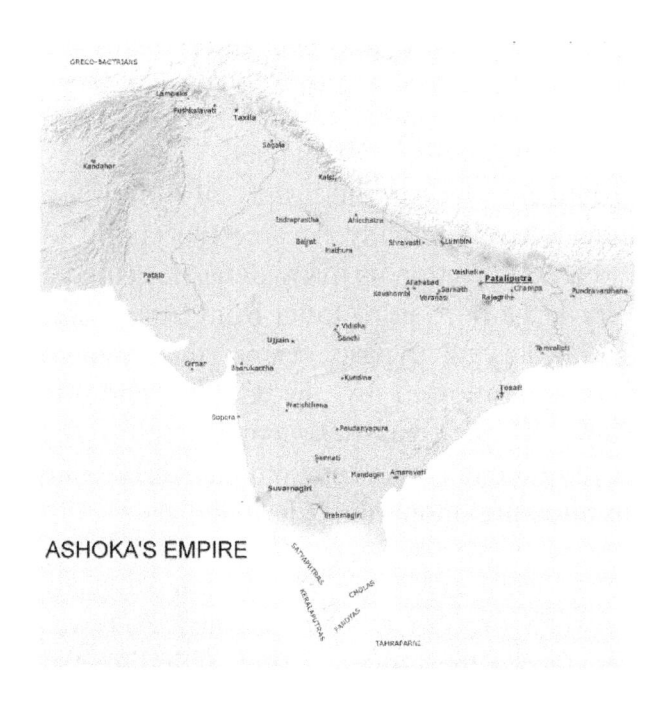

ASHOKA'S EMPIRE

The history of the place was usually etched on the pillar in the *Brahmi lipi*. There are no ruins connected with the times of the Buddha at Pataliputra as Buddha never stayed here, but there are ruins of the palace of Ashoka at a place called Kumrahar. Buddha's physician Jivaka lived at Pataliputra, and there are ruins of his place of work at Kumrahar. A huge broken Ashoka Pillar can also be seen near the ruins of the palace which was largely made of wood.

Pataliputra remained a very prominent place in the history of India for a long time. It actually became the cradle of Indian civilisation as many dynasties ruled a very large portion of India from here. After the Mauryan dynasty came the Shunga dynasty followed by the Guptas and the Palas. These dynasties contributed to the development of sculpture, art and architectural monuments in India.

The rule of the Gupta dynasty between the 4th and 5th century AD was considered the golden period of India. Art, architecture, literature were given a lot of importance and encouragement by the rulers.

LUMBINI to KUSHINARA

The great poet Kalidas and the Astronomer Aryabhatta lived in these times.

HUGE BROKEN ASHOKA PILLAR

THE BUDDHA

14

BUDDHA'S COUNTENANCE

Do we know what Buddha really looked like? Till about the 1st century AD no statues of the Buddha had been made. Buddha was worshipped through aniconic objects which meant that certain symbols were used; such as the stupa, the *Bodhi* tree, the wheel of *dhamma*, an empty throne or footprints. This later culminated in iconic worship when his first statues were made around 1st century AD, at Gandhar, which is now in Afghanistan. There was Greco Bactrian influence on art then and Buddha's depiction may have been according to the artistic imagination of the creator of the sculpture. The features of Buddha are aquiline, and the clothes draping his shoulders are like the robes worn by the Greeks.

GANDHAR BUDDHA

Gandhar and Mathura were the two capitals of the Kushana empire during the 1st century AD, where art, architecture and sculpting was developed. We find a number of statues of the Buddha made either at Gandhar or at Mathura.

After these statues were commissioned, art of making the statues of Buddha flourished. He was mostly shown seated with his hand in different postures or *mudras,* where every *mudra* conveyed a different meaning.

In Afghanistan in the 6th century AD, there were huge statues of the Buddha made in a place called Bamiyan. These statues were destroyed by the Taliban in 2001. Bamiyan lies on the ancient Silk Route which was a caravan route linking China with the West. There were a number of monasteries here housing about one thousand monks, as was stated by Hiuen Tsang who visited this place in 630 AD. Most probably "*But parasti*" which means praying to statues could have been derived from the word Buddha which could have got distorted as "But" over a period of time.

It is interesting to note that most statues of the Buddha were made from 1st century AD to 5th century AD. They were mainly made at Mathura, Gandhar and Bharhut.

The face that we see and the statues that we see of the Buddha have all been developed much after his death and at places far away from where he lived, therefore we really do not know what Buddha looked like.

15

6th CENTURY BC

The last couple of centuries, from the 18th century to the present day have been very progressive times. There were many inventions and discoveries made which changed the way of life of human beings. Scientific invention, innovation, development and also a revolution in the means of communication and transport came about. In the same way, 6th Century BC was also witness to a number of radical changes in thoughts and philosophy which brought about a revolutionary change in the lives of the people of those times.

While Buddha lived in India from 563 BC to 483 BC, another thinker named Mahavir also lived in India. Mahavir was born near Vaishali in Bihar in 599 BC and died in 527 BC in Pawapuri, also near Vaishali. Mahavir was the 24th and last Tirthankara of the Jains.

Around the same time Confucius was another philosopher who lived in China from 551 BC to 479 BC. He was a teacher, editor, politician and philosopher. He emphasized personal and governmental morality, correctness of social relationships, justice and sincerity.

In Greece, Pythagoras was born in Samos Island in 570 BC. He was a Mathematician and Philosopher.

Zoroaster(628-551 BC) taught his philosophy in Persia.

Aesop, whose fables are known all over the world is also said to have lived in this century from 620 BC to 564 BC in Greece. Aesop was a slave who had won his freedom. The characters in his fables were animals and inanimate objects that spoke, solved problems and had human characteristics. We in India had a similar kind of story teller in Vishnu Sharma who wrote the "*Panchatantra*", where the characters were birds and animals. *Panchatantra* however did not belong to 6th Century BC. *Panchatantra* was written in the 3rd century BC.

The massive Temple of Zeus, had been started in 520 BC, in Athens Greece, but the work was stopped after the base platform and columns had been erected and remained incomplete for 336 years. Zeus was one of the twelve Olympians of Greek religion and mythology. Architecture and the skill to design and build a temple of this magnitude was already developed in Greece.

In Persia Cyrus and Darius had already started expansion of their empire. Cyrus annexed the Greek territory of

Ionia as part of his Empire and also captured Babylon. In India, Greece is often referred to as "Yavan", this could be a colloquial form of the word Ionia.

Susruta a physician of India developed surgery. Indian medical theory introduced the thought that the human body consisted of three elements, spirit, phlegm and bile.

The Hanging Gardens of Babylon were made in the 6th Century BC.

In Greece the Isthmian games at Corinth were begun in 582 BC, the Pythian Games were also begun and were held at Delphi. These games also included competition in art and dance.

Democracy was beginning to take shape. When Solon of Greece was elected Archon or Chief magistrate, he cancelled the debts of the peasants of Attica and made it illegal to enslave a debtor. He made every citizen a member of the Ecclesia, which was responsible for election of the Archon.

Later in 507 BC Cleisthenes, who was brought to power by popular support gave every Athenian a voice in the demos, which was the local council at village or town level. He also began random selection of citizens to fill government positions, rather than select people based on heredity and kinship. He increased the power of the Athenian Citizen's Assembly and reduced the power of the nobility.

6th Century BC was therefore a century which saw the advent of many thinkers, reformists, philosophers, and writers across Asia. Out of all these, the philosophy of Buddha has spread all over the world like sunshine which brightens up the world in every corner, every day.

EPILOGUE

Siddharth who began his journey of life at Lumbini, lived for eighty years. His journey ended at Kushinara. At the age of 29 he left the comforts of his home and after six years of wandering, finding teachers to enhance his knowledge and practicing strict meditation, he found answers and solutions to his quest.

What exact words did he use in his sermons are not known to us, but we know that he believed that every human being was equal, and that there could be no discrimination between people on any basis. He believed that each person controlled his own fate or destiny and it was not in the control of any other being. He believed that every person should treat everyone else with compassion, tolerance and an attitude of forgiveness.

Each person was asked to question and not believe anything blindly. Superstition and blind faith would therefore be eradicated and human beings would be empowered. Once a person is able to use his own power of reasoning, he can convince himself to follow what he thinks is right. Everything in moderation leads to a life with less strife and struggle.

Buddha's philosophy came down through word of mouth. Bhikku Anand was the master of *Dhamma* and Bhikku Upali was the master of *Vinaya* and they recited these *suttas* at the First *Sangiti* after Buddha's death. Over a period of time different interpretations of the philosophy of Buddhism has taken place.

What remains important is the basic philosophy which is, "*Atta deep bhava*" which means be your own light. Think, evaluate and then believe. If one follows this thought process, then we can find our own right path to follow.

Buddha's philosophy spoke of *Aniccha*, which means that everything is subject to change. The philosophy itself is subject to change. That is the reason why his philosophy has stood the test of time. It was not laid down for posterity to follow blindly.

The essence of this philosophy is that nothing remains permanent. Life itself is mortal. Change is the essence of life.

There are only two universal truths in this world which are not subject to change. One is that the sun rises in the east. The second is that every being that is born has to die.

As you and I have travelled together from Lumbini to Kushinara and a little beyond too, I hope you enjoyed this journey with me through the thick forests of the 6th century BC to the modern age of the 21st century AD, where the eternally changing world continuously gives us new challenges to face every day. Taking charge of our own life, trusting our own decisions, living without fear of the unknown would enhance the quality of our life.

In the end I too say, "*Atta Deep Bhava*".

Varsha Uke Nagpal

BUDDHA 2nd CENTURY AD
GANDHAR

BUDDHIST CONFERENCE/ *SANGITI*

There were six Buddhist conferences held after the death of Buddha where different issues relating to the teachings of the Buddha were discussed. *Sangiti* is sam+giti which means reciting together. In the Buddhist context, it means the recitation of the teachings of the Buddha for their collection, compilation, classification, verification, approval and memorization.

THE FIRST *SANGITI* - 483 BC

It was held at Saptaprni Caves in Rajgrih, under the patronage of Ajatshatru with the

Bhikku Mahakasyapa presiding. Upali recited the *Vinaya* while Anand recited the *Suttas* pertaining to *Dhamma*. It was decided that all the rules would remain as there was no dispute and the teachings had remained unchanged. There were 500 bhikkus who attended this *Sangiti* and agreed with the decisions taken.

THE SECOND *SANGITI* - 383 BC
It was held at Vaishali under the patronage of Kalashoka.
Seven hundred monks attended this *Sangiti* where rules of *Vinaya* were discussed.

THIRD *SANGITI* - 250 BC
This was held at Pataliputra under the patronage of King Ashoka and was presided over by Tissa. 1000 monks attended this *Sangiti*. This *sangiti* was called to rid the *Sangha* of corruption and bogus monks.

FOURTH *SANGITI* – 29 BC
This was held at Tambapanni in Srilanka under the patronage of King Vattagamani. At this *Sangiti* the entire *Tripitaka* was written down, as it was recited by 500 monks. This was according to Theravad tradition.
Another Sangiti, also called Fourth Sangiti is said to have taken place in 78 AD at

Kuntalvana, Kashmir, presided by Vasumitra, under patronage of King Kanishka, according to the Sarvastivada tradition.

FIFTH *SANGITI* - 1871 AD

This was held at Mandalay in Myanmar. The objective was to examine the teachings of the Buddha in minute detail and to ensure that no distortions had crept in the teachings. 2400 monks took part in this *Sangiti*.

SIXTH *SANGITI* - 1954 AD

This was held at Yangon in Myanmar. It was sponsored by the Myanmar government. 2500 monks from eight countries attended this *Sangiti*, where teachings of the Buddha were examined to ensure that there was no distortion.

LUMBINI to KUSHINARA

ASHOKA'S STONE EDICT

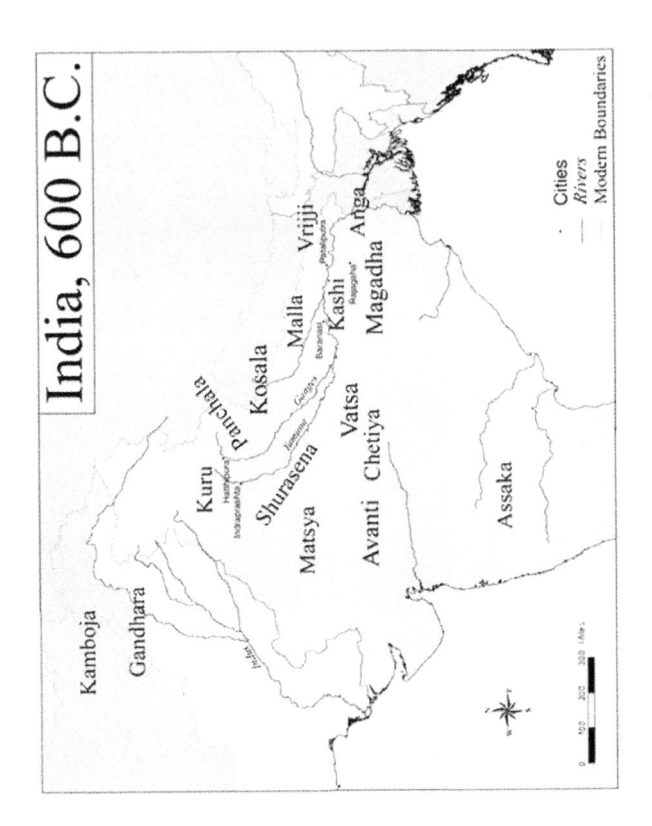

GANARAJYAS

6th CENTURY BC

16 GANARAJYAS

There were a few Monarchies in those days. Most prominent were Anga, Avanti, Kosala, Magadh and Vatsa. Later some of these also became *ganarajyas*.

There were sixteen *Ganarajyas* where the King was elected.

NAME (then)	NAME (now)	RIVER
Assaka	Near Godavari	Godavari
Anga	Bhagalpur	Champa
Avanti	Malwa	Vetravati
Chedi	Bundelkhand	Vetravati

NAME (then)	NAME (now)	RIVER
Gandhar	East Afghanistan	Indus
Kashi	Varanasi	Ganga
Kamboj	Rajouri	Tawi
Kuru	Thanesar	Yamuna
Koshal	Shrawasti	Gandak
Magadh	Patna	Ganga
Malla	Kushinagar	Kakuttha
Matsya	Jaipur	Sahibi
Panchal	Farrukhabad	Ganga
Surasena	Mathura	Yamuna
Vriji	Vaishali	Ganga
Vatsa	Allahabad	Ganga

First Five Disciples of Buddha:

1. Kaundinya
2. Kasyapa.
3. Mahanama
4. Asvajit
5. Bhaduka

MAPS IN THE BOOK

	Page
Buddha's Path	6
Gangetic Plain	16
Ashoka's Empire	129
Ganarajyas - 6th Century BC	152

GLOSSARY

Abhishek – purification.
Anand kuti - The Happy Cottage.
Anath pindika - Saviour of orphans.
Angulimala – Garland of fingers/name of person.
Aniccha – Impermanence.
Arhat - One who is worthy.
Ashtang marg - Eight fold path.
Atta deep bhava - Be your own light.
Bhikku - A monk.
Bikkhu Sangh - Community of male monks.
Bhikkuni Sangh - Community of women monks.
Bhiksha patra - Begging bowl.
Brahmi - script prevalent in 3rd BC to 5th century AD.
Bodhi - another name for *peepal* tree.
Brahmin - the priestly caste in Hinduism.
But parasti – idol worship.

Chaitya – A Buddhist shrine or a prayer hall with a stupa at one end.

Chunar – A kind of reddish or buff coloured hard sandstone from a place called Chunar.

Dhamma – Religion.

Dharma chakra parivartan - Setting in motion the wheel of religion for change.

Dhyanic - type of meditation.

Dukkha – suffering, sorrow.

Dwarpal - Gate keeper.

Ganarajya - Republic.

Gandha kuti - The perfumed Cottage.

Gandhikanama - Currency of the Perfumery guild.

Gaya - gone.

Himalaya - The abode of snow.

Kacchi kuti - Temporary cottage.

Kalama Sutta / Kessaputtiya Sutta - Discourse on free thought and questioning given at Kesariya town.

Kheer - Rice pudding.

Kshatriya - Warrior Caste.

Lipi – script.

Mahabharata - An epic about a war that took place in ancient India.

Mahaparinirvana - refers to death of Buddha.

Mudra - hand gesture.

Mula-gandha Kuti - Cottage with fragrance.

Nagar vadhu - Bride of the town.

Niti - policy.

Pakki kuti - Permanent Cottage.

Panchatantra - Collection of moralistic stories with animal characters.

Parampara - Tradition.

Parinirvana - death of an enlightened person.

Parivrajaka - Wandering monk.

Peepal - Tree (Ficus Religiosa).

Purnima - Full moon night.

Ranchhod - Deserter from war.

Saal - Tree (Shorea Robusta).

Samner - a novice monk.

Sangha - Organised group with common interest.

Sangiti – Conference, reciting together.

Santhagara - Assembly place.

Shankh lipi - A type of ancient script.

Shishya - student.

Shradh - funeral rite.

Shreshti - merchant.

Shudra - the caste that served the other three castes.

Swarn bhandar - Golden Treasure House.

Tantricism - Ancient Indian tradition of beliefs and meditation and ritual practices.

Terai - Wetland.

Tonga - Horse drawn carriage.

Tongawala - Driver of horse drawn carriage.

Tripitaka - Buddhist scripture.

Vaishakh - April or May months in Gregorian Callender.

Vaishakh Purnima - Full moon night in the month of Vaishakh.

Varshavaas - Stay during monsoon.

Venuvan - Bamboo grove.

Vinaya - Discipline.

Vriksha devata - Tree God.

LUMBINI to KUSHINARA

VARSHA

Varsha loves travelling and visiting new places. She loves to read about the place which she plans to visit, so that she knows the history of the place and knows what she should see and explore. Her travels have taken her far and wide around the world.

Varsha has always been fond of reading and began writing after she retired from her job with a Bank, which she had joined as a Probationary Officer in 1975.

This is her first book in this genre where she undertakes a journey into the times of the 6th century BC.